My First
Disney
READY SET LEARN!
Activity Pad
Develop your child's literacy, numeracy and fine motor skills with these fun, educational and magical activities!
This symbol indicates there is something to trace on the page with your finger.
Colour in the picture when you see this symbol.
AF585404

GROWN-UPS
Help your child to trace over the lines with their finger.

PRE-WRITING PRACTICE

TRACE THE LINES WITH YOUR FINGER

Join Pegasus to trace along the lines using your finger.

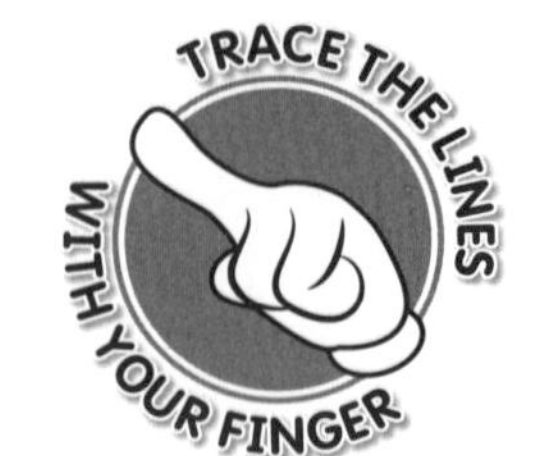

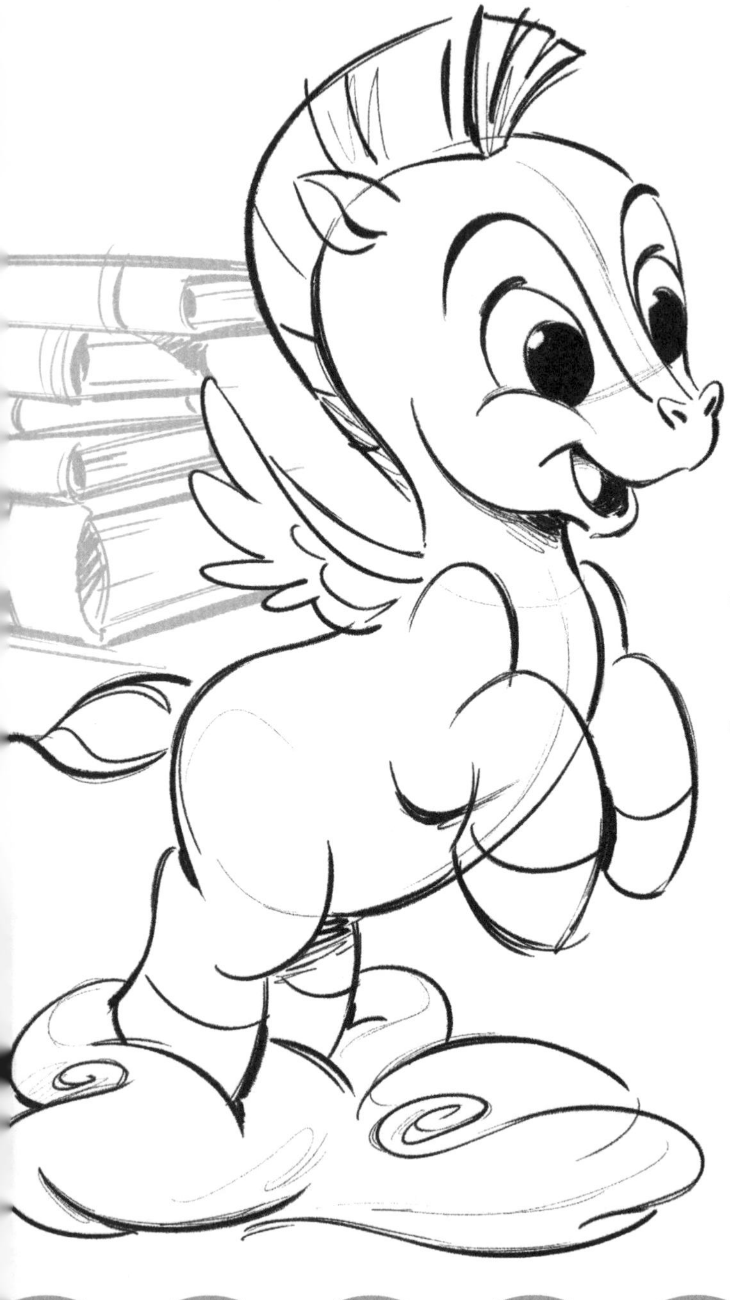

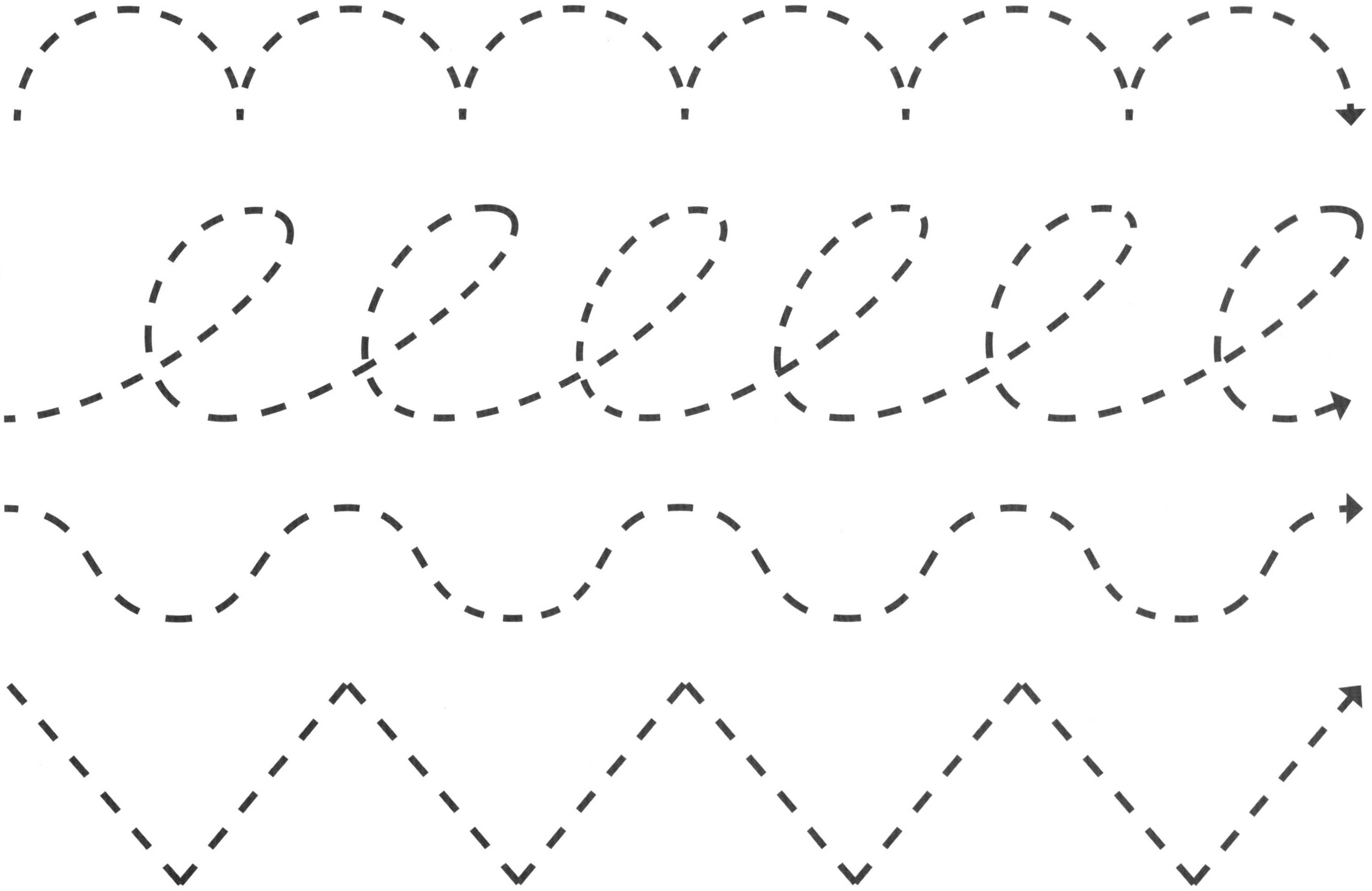

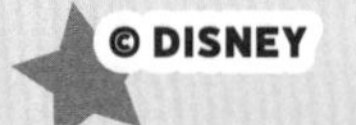

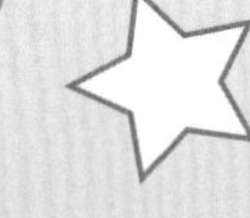

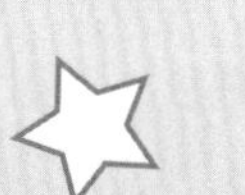

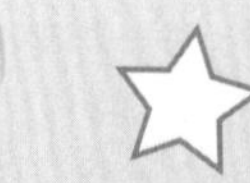

Aa
A is for Ant.
GROWN-UPS
Help your child to trace over the lines with their finger.
Bb
B is for Bee.
a
b
TRACE THE LINES WITH YOUR FINGER
TRACE THE LINES WITH YOUR FINGER
Try saying words with the letter A.
Can you draw an apple?
COLOUR IN THE PICTURE
apple
Alice
Try saying words with the letter B.
bird
bunny
© DISNEY

Cc
C is for Castle.
GROWN-UPS
Try making big letter C shapes in the air together.
TRACE THE LINES WITH YOUR FINGER
Try saying words with the letter C.
Can you colour Olaf's carrot
nose orange?
COLOUR IN THE PICTURE
carrot
cat
Dd
D is for Dad.
TRACE THE LINES WITH YOUR FINGER
Try saying words with the letter D.
Give Snow White's deer a name!
deer
Dory

Ee
E is for Elephant.
GROWN-UPS
Help your children name as many friends as they can.
TRACE THE LINES WITH YOUR FINGER
Try saying words with the letter E.
COLOUR IN THE PICTURE
Eric
eel
Try saying words with the letter F.
frog
flowers
Ff
F is for Friend.
TRACE THE LINES WITH YOUR FINGER

Gg

G is for Gold.

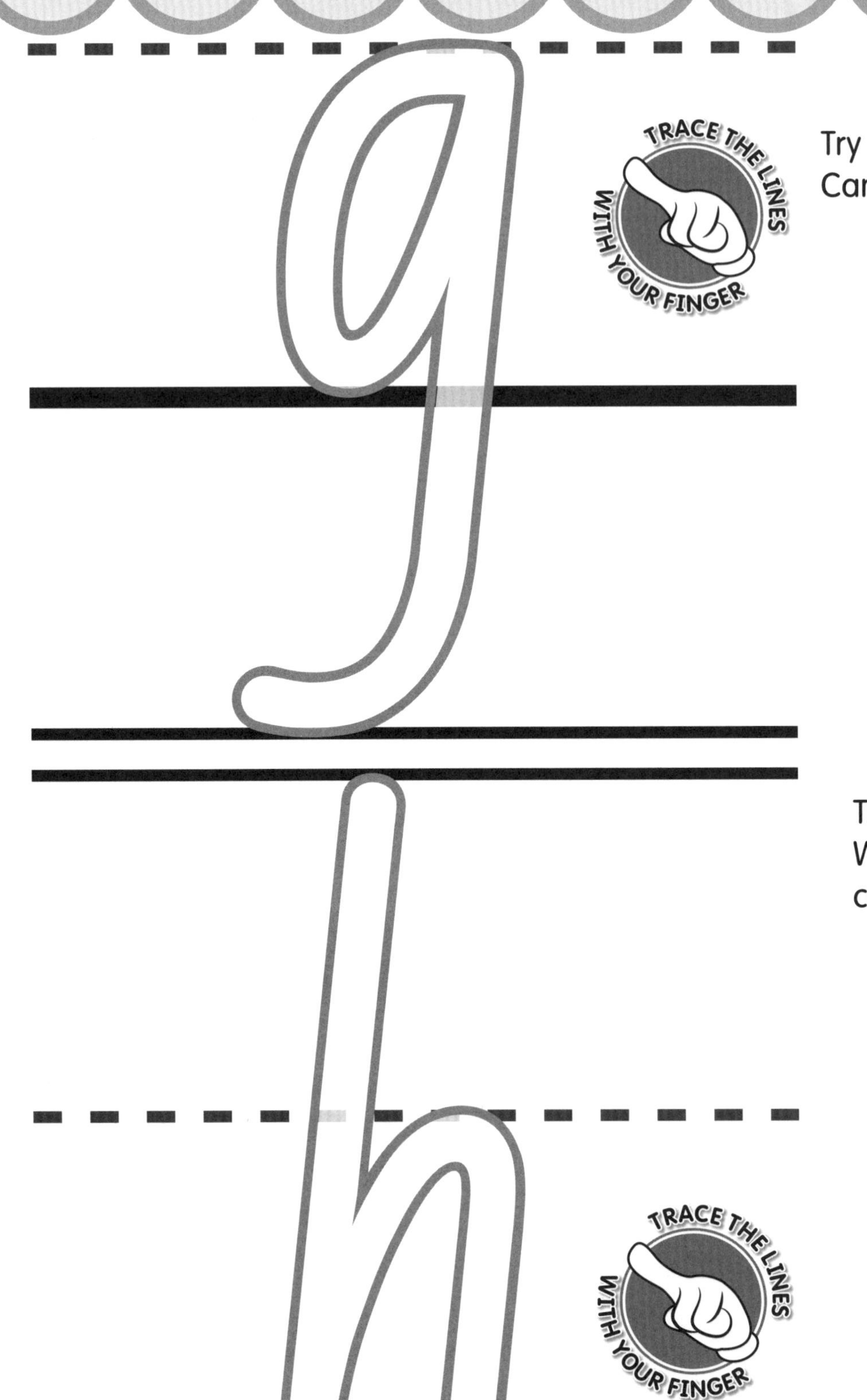

Try saying words with the letter G.
Can you point to Carl's glasses?

Grumpy

glasses

Hh

H is for House.

Try saying words with the letter H.
What colour is Merida's long curly hair?

hairbrush

hair

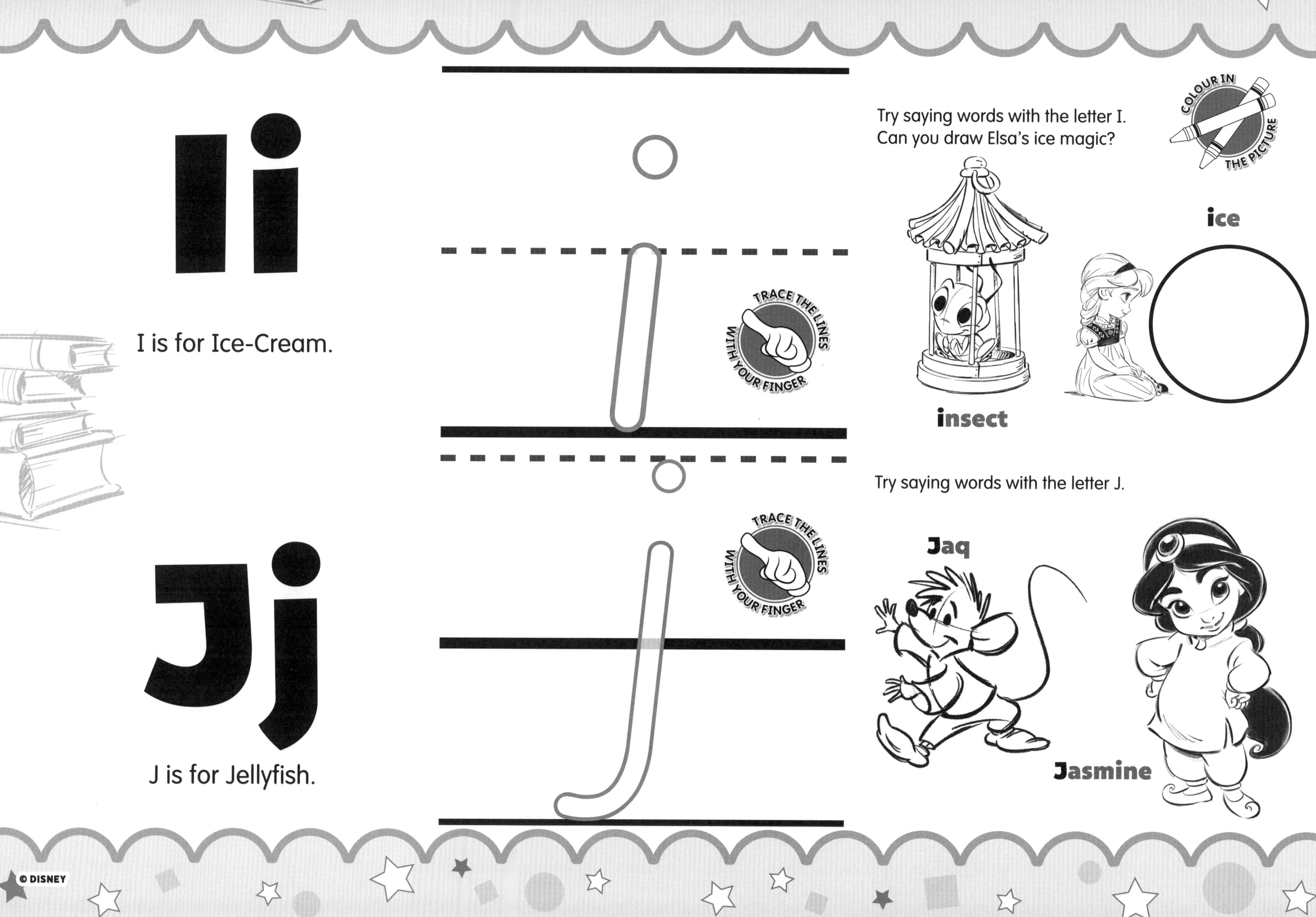
Ii
I is for Ice-Cream.
TRACE THE LINES WITH YOUR FINGER
Try saying words with the letter I.
Can you draw Elsa's ice magic?
COLOUR IN THE PICTURE
ice
insect
Jj
J is for Jellyfish.
TRACE THE LINES WITH YOUR FINGER
Try saying words with the letter J.
Jaq
Jasmine
© DISNEY

Kk

K is for King.

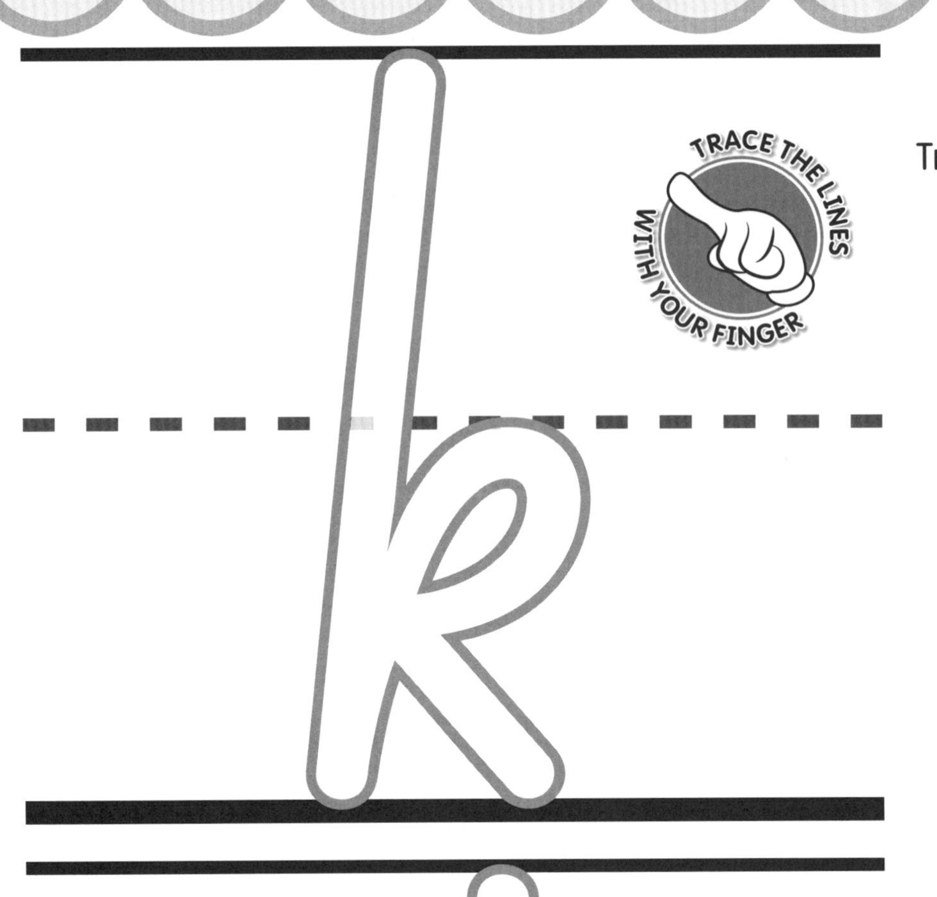

Try saying words with the letter K.

kick

Kristoff

Ll

L is for Lion.

Try saying words with the letter L.

Lilo

lantern

Mm

M is for Monkey.

Nn

N is for Nest.

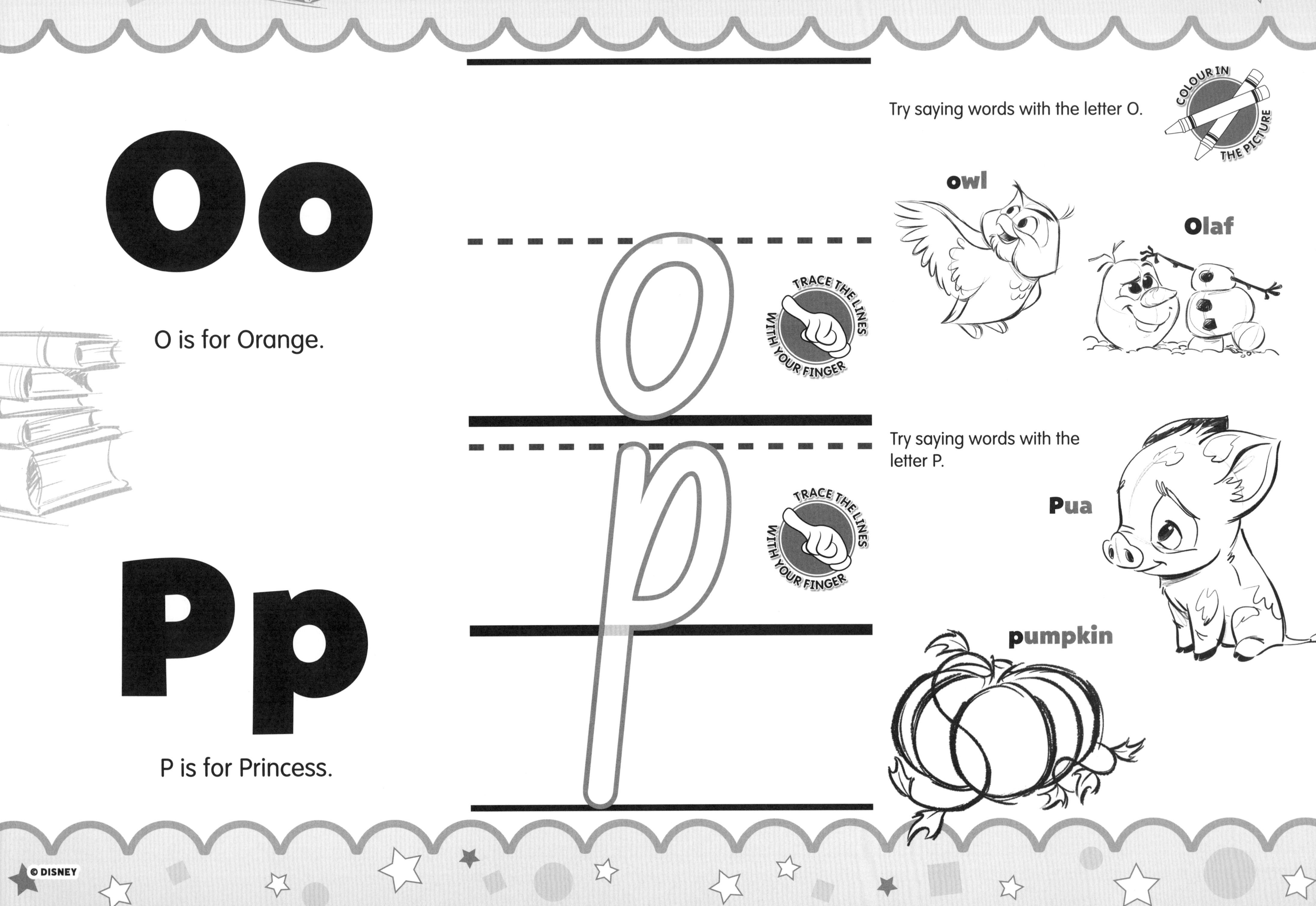
Oo
O is for Orange.
Pp
P is for Princess.
o
TRACE THE LINES WITH YOUR FINGER
p
TRACE THE LINES WITH YOUR FINGER
Try saying words with the letter O.
COLOUR IN THE PICTURE
owl
Olaf
Try saying words with the letter P.
Pua
pumpkin
© DISNEY

Qq
Q is for Queen.
GROWN-UPS
A fun way to recreate the letters is moulding playdough over the shape.
TRACE THE LINES WITH YOUR FINGER
Try saying words with the letter Q.
Can you point to Tiana's crown
that's fit for a queen?
COLOUR IN THE PICTURE
Queen's crown
quick
Rr
R is for Rabbit.
TRACE THE LINES WITH YOUR FINGER
Try saying words with the letter R.
What colour should Cinderella's ribbon be?
rose
ribbon
© DISNEY

Ss

S is for Swimming.

Try saying words with the letter S.

TRACE THE LINES WITH YOUR FINGER

Tt

T is for Turtle.

TRACE THE LINES WITH YOUR FINGER

Try saying words with the letter T.

Uu

U is for Umbrella.

GROWN-UPS
Make up fun ways to trace–try using your thumb, fist, foot or nose!

u

TRACE THE LINES WITH YOUR FINGER

Try saying words with the letter U.

COLOUR IN THE PICTURE

Under

Mulan

Try saying words with the letter V.

Vv

V is for Violin.

v

TRACE THE LINES WITH YOUR FINGER

Vanellope

villain

Ww

W is for Water.

Try saying words with the letter W.

spinning wheel

Wendy

Xx

X is for Xylophone.

Try saying words with the letter X.

Max

explore

Yy
Y is for Yo-yo.
GROWN-UPS
Ask your little one to think of more words starting with 'Z'.
TRACE THE LINES WITH YOUR FINGER
Try saying words with the letter Y.
COLOUR IN THE PICTURE
fly
Dopey
Try saying words with the letter Z.
zig-zag
Zz
TRACE THE LINES WITH YOUR FINGER
Z is for Zebra.
Rapunzel
© DISNEY

1
I Carriage.
COLOUR IN THE PICTURE
Trace the lines of Cinderella's carriage!
TRACE THE LINES WITH YOUR FINGER

2

2 Ears.

Can you count this bunny's ears?

3 Bears.

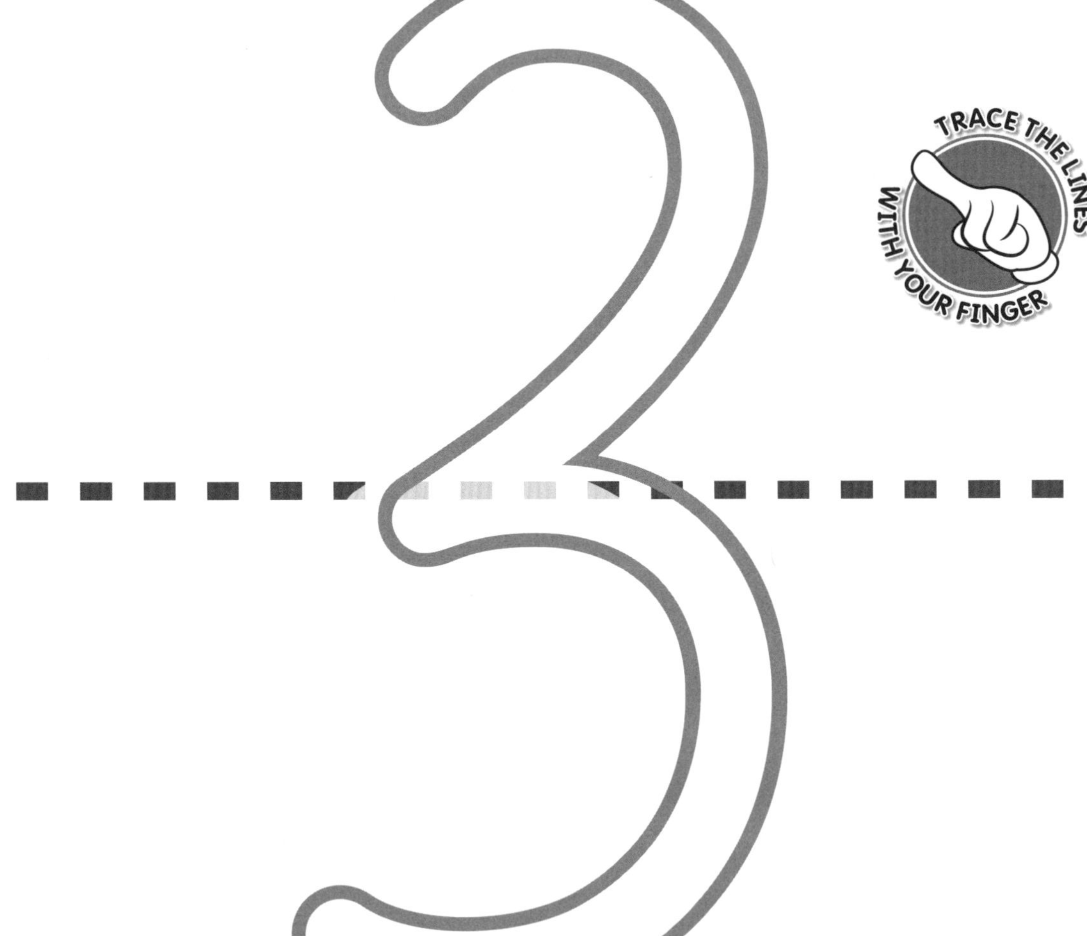

Can you count three bears?

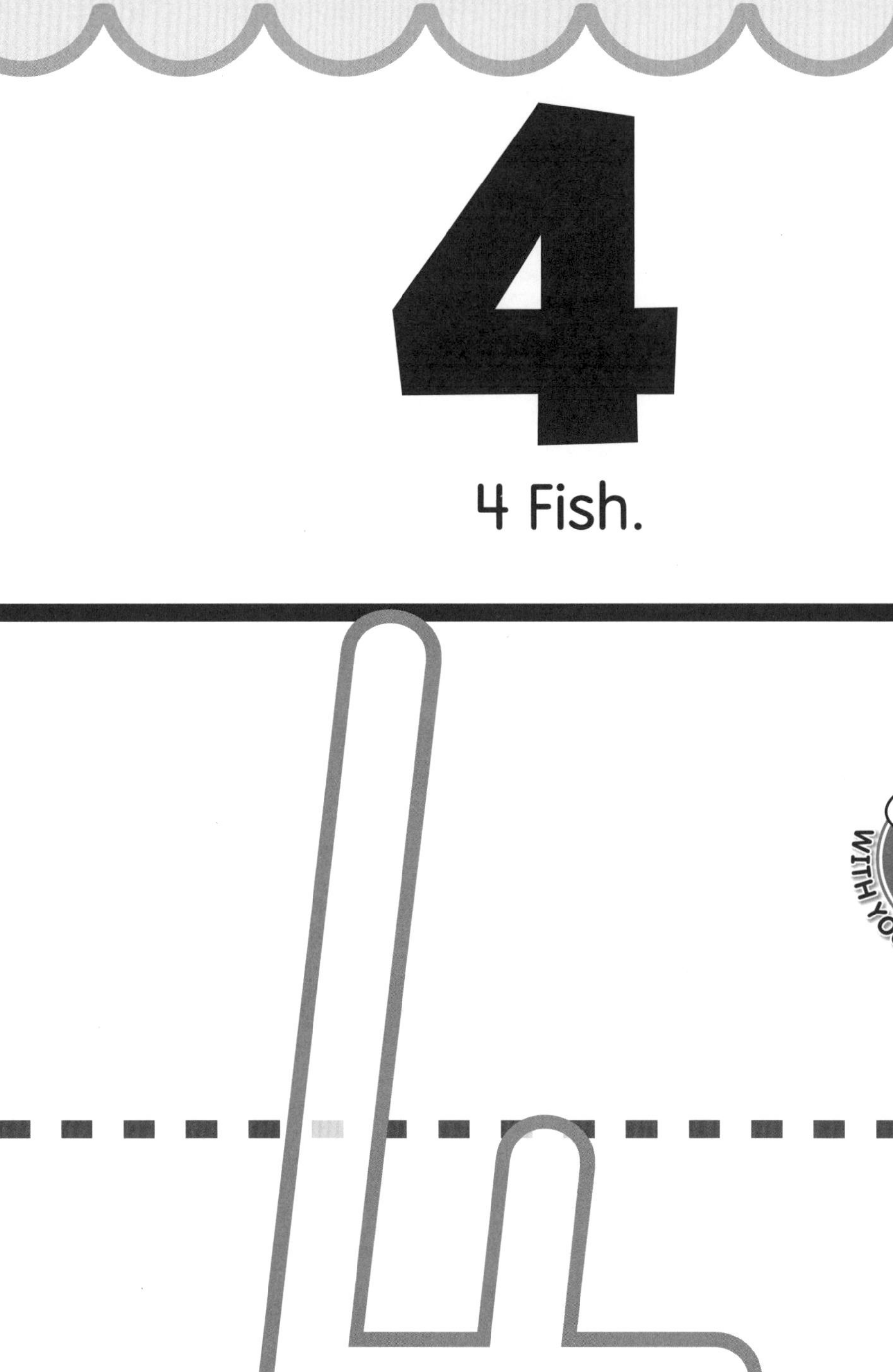

4 Fish.

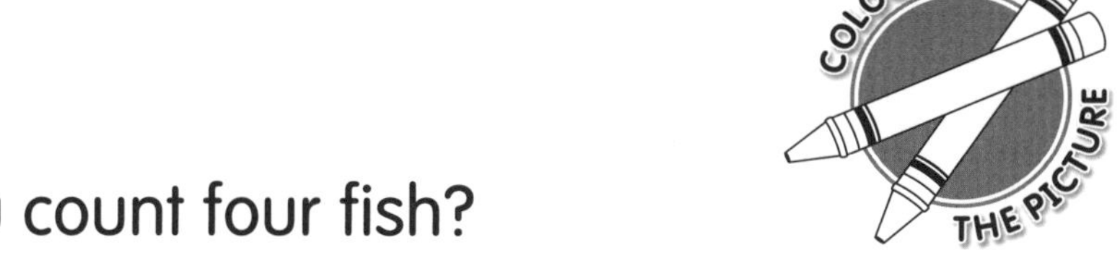

Can you count four fish?

5 Books.

Can you count this stack of books?

SHAPE IDENTIFICATION

Anna is looking for a circle! Point to the circle and trace its shape. Can you name some things around your house that are also a circle?

FEATURE FINDING

Can you point to these facial features on Aladdin?
Find them on your own face too!

GROWN-UPS
Help your child point to the features they share with Aladdin.

nose

eyes

hair

eyebrow

lips

teeth

USE YOUR SENSES

Ask your child these questions to help them use their senses

1 I use my eyes to see.
Can you blink your eyes?
I did it!

2 I use my nose to smell.
Can you sniff with your nose?
I did it!

3 I use my ears to hear.
Can you touch your ears?
I did it!

4 I use my tongue to taste.
Can you stick out your tongue?
I did it!

5 I use my hands to touch.
Can you touch your hands together?
I did it!

GROWN-UPS
Help your little one name their best friends.

THE BEST OF FRIENDS

Look at these best friends below. Say their names, and say 'chicken' when you spot Heihei!

Moana and Heihei

Mulan and Mushu

Pocahontas and Meeko

Lilo and Stitch

Hercules and Pegasus

Eric and Max